For the wise leader that lies dormant in us all

Ceannas Publishing 2021
www.ceannas.com

# FOREWORD

I am honoured to write the introduction to this remarkable book of poetry "The Poetry of Leadership: The Wisdom of Knowing you Know Nothing", written by Don Ledingham of Ceannas, and so meaningfully designed by Gary Haston.

I'm of the generation which at school listened in silence. We were not encouraged to think for ourselves, to wonder or debate.

It wasn't until I was fortunate enough to be taught by Mr Gunn, a remarkable teacher at Hamilton Academy, who opened my eyes to poetry where we discussed what the poet's words meant.

Eighty years later, one of his favourite sayings remains with me:

"Poetry is thoughts that breathe, and words that burn." Thomas Gray

This was subsequently reinforced by W.H. Auden's words:

"Poetry is when an emotion has found its thought, and the thought has found words."

In a world that seems to place a premium on facts and numbers over feelings and emotions; technical information over imagination and passion; and process and mechanics over wonder and inspiration, perhaps it is time to reflect on a concept such as leadership through the medium of poetry as captured by Gray and Auden?

The power of poetry is its capacity to capture the essence of complex issues. Poetry is language at its most condensed and most potent.

It is my belief that the words in this book fulfil that obligation to capture the essence of leadership, and escape from our tendency to over-elaborate and complicate.

I hope it will encourage the reader to wonder about leadership and about themselves as leaders and that it will lead to debate - what could be more important?


Sir Charles Fraser

# CONTENTS

| | | | | |
|---|---|---|---|---|
| Wisdom | 6 | Scales of imagination | 31 |
| Candour | 8 | Remembering the future | 32 |
| Creativity | 9 | I am a fortress | 33 |
| Cynic | 10 | A force of nature | 34 |
| Daydreaming | 11 | Are you the best friend that you could have? | 36 |
| Empathy | 12 | Fear of my light going out | 37 |
| Exposure | 13 | To see ourselves | 38 |
| Hilltop people | 14 | The chief executive | 39 |
| Imagination | 16 | Tugging at a loosened thread | 40 |
| Integrity | 17 | Better to be roughly right | 41 |
| Nothing always does | 18 | Belonging | 42 |
| Obliquity | 19 | The analyst | 43 |
| Inspiration | 20 | The difference between knowing and understanding | 44 |
| Trust | 21 | The leader's sacrifice | 45 |
| Beautiful mistakes | 22 | The time borrower | 46 |
| Friendly fire | 23 | Uncertainty | 47 |
| She only saw the light | 24 | Vulnerable invulnerability | 48 |
| Your word | 25 | Adaptability | 49 |
| Milestones | 26 | Waves against the wind | 50 |
| A map is not the territory | 27 | An inconvenient truth | 51 |
| Whatever normal is? | 28 | Leadership: poetry or plumbing | 52 |
| Seeing for ourselves | 29 | | |
| Who did you plan to be? | 30 | | |

# WISDOM

The fool will rarely listen
Preferring through omission
To fill the space of thoughtful hush,
With lines that start with I;
The wise prefer to listen
As a time for acquisition
And only speak to understand,
And ask the reasons why;

The fool blindly follows others
Where shared opinions smother
Thoughts that go against the grain,
Of mainstream status quo;
The wise don't heed convention
And have no apprehension
Before they set in motion,
Thoughts that tip a domino;

The fool takes no correction
And sees it as rejection
A personal attack that
Dents shallow confidence;
The wise don't fear objection
And seek interrogation
If it generates ideas,
Of greater consequence;

The fool hoards information
As a means of confirmation
That rank has been achieved
And that power is retained;
The wise set out to distribute
To see their knowledge contribute
And carry wisdom lightly,
As if it were the wind;

The fool lives in the present
Takes no account of dissent
And is driven by self-interest
And absence of respect;
The wise look back and forwards
To the past and to the future
Seeing them as one,
And making them connect;

For fools are sadly destined
To lead their lives unquestioned
And see themselves correct,
In everything they do;
Yet the wise who seem uncertain
And who never cease to question
Will lead the more fulfilling life,
Where all they do is true.

# CANDOUR

Candour slides both ways,
Drifting between the cruelty
And purity of Truth,
The weapon of choice,
For those who only
See through selfish eyes,
Or a mirror
On one's life
Which never lies
And keeps us true
To whom we wish to be.

# CREATIVITY

We change our world,
With the power of ideas;
Which gently lift to view,
Like quiet sunrise,
Diminishing the shadows,
In gradual revelation;
Or softly grow,
Through passing days,
Nourished by the soil,
Tended into life,
By careful hands;
Or simply beaten into being,
All smoke and noise,
Shaped and formed,
Then tempered in the forge;
Yet see that instant,
Where life takes hold,
Where moments earlier,
None existed,
In vitro of the mind, synapsed,
Arcing across divides,
Our own Large Hadron Collider,
Hurtling idle thoughts,
Towards each other,
Ever accelerating, until,
Exploding fragments coalesce,
Changing our world,
One particle,
At a time.

# CYNIC

Beware!
Bitterness,
Can foul your soul.
Its brackish taste
Lends acrid flavour
To the sweetest dish.
Twisting smile to sneer
To feed off
Blame and scorn,
As envy and contempt,
Infecting with their bile,
Give jaundiced eyes their proof.
Until,
It turns on itself.
And eats us from within.

# DAYDREAMING

Pushing through the undergrowth of the present
She made a clearing amongst the tallest trees,
And once hidden from view she left herself behind;
Lifting off, gradually, inch by inch, rising,
High above the canopy: not flying, just lifting;
Higher and higher; effortlessly,
Into the unoccupied space;
While others struggle, manfully,
Occupied with the serious business
Of work, mindful of the here and now;
Leaving her to her indulgence
Her idle reveries, which leave no trace
Upon the here and now,
Yet creating a future,
Far beyond the reach
Of those who
Despise her flighting
Dreams.

# EMPATHY

To step inside another
To step outside yourself
To have the power to project
To be someone other than 'myself'.

For some it is a short step
For others more a leap
Yet others feel they get there
When all they do is weep.

For many there is comfort
They pretend when others feel
They have pity and sincerity
And say that time will heal.

But I prefer the notion
Much more than words or deed
That it's more to do with sharing
Much more than hearts that bleed.

To celebrate with others
Their victories and success
Is more difficult than pity
If they have more than you possess.

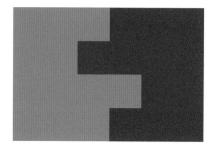

# EXPOSURE

Have you ever stood on deck
And tried to shelter from anxiety's biting wind,
Broken from routine's comfort
And felt the stinging spray of isolation?
Or stepped out all but naked
And heard ridicule's distant thunder,
And lost your way
Forced to walk,
Bent forwards,
Into the gathering storm?
Or weighed anchor
Thinking danger's squall had passed,
To find yourself alone
As falling pressure banks the fog?
I have stood there,
Stand there,
Times.
Amidst jeopardy's shifting ice pack.
Confidence floating just above the waves
Self-doubt,
Lurking,
Just below
The waterline.

# HILLTOP PEOPLE

Do not pass the hillside road worth climbing,
Despite temptations of the valley floor,
For level journeys seem so forgiving
When faced with what appears a half-shut door,
But see it as a welcome chance, well found,
And make your start towards that hidden place,
To leave behind the safe yet shaded ground,
Where live those timid souls who leave no trace,
Then feel your pounding heart and muscles burn,
And question, surely, such a reckless act,
But soon you pass that point of no return,
Where such quiet ambition becomes a fact,
To stand and gaze upon a wondrous land,
A view that only hilltop people understand.

# IMAGINATION

That magic moment in the morning
As dreams and thoughts exchange,
Indistinguishable,
Bending at the edges,
Distorted by the gravity
Of my imagination,
Where nothing is impossible
Where nothing ever dies,
Where nothing, ever,
Lies.

# INTEGRITY

Such a fragile thread
In which to place
Our lifetime's trust,
A tenuous cord, which can,
Without attention,
Fray and wear
Through our neglect,
And indiscretions,
Yet see it break,
Hear its elemental snap,
For us to fall to earth,
That no witness
Need observe,
For public laws and rules,
Are weak compared
To our reproach,
Which holds us upright
In our ascent,
And upon which,
Too late to notice,
Only we,
Rely.

# NOTHING
# ALWAYS DOES

Breathe out,
Step back,
Admire a job well done,
Accept the applause,
But the first
Faltering steps
To complacency,
Begin with that desire
For the world,
To stop turning.
Just to lay your head
A moment, on the soft
Cushions of achievement,
Only to wake up,
Too late to learn that,
"Nothing always does".

# OBLIQUITY

We learn to walk
One step following another,
And so we see this
As the way to reach
Our destinations,
In straight lines
From here to there,
Following our compass,
Connecting the dots
In logical linearity,
Yet in our heart of hearts
We know the folly
Of straight lines,
For successful journeys
Rarely follow
Well-trodden routes,
Instead remember
The unintentioned arrival
At that special place
Which opens out in front of us,
Surprising us with our luck,
So break free from
The tyranny of rational roads,
Of safety's small-minded steps,
And jump instead,
From stone to stone,
Leap chasms,
Navigate the swamps,
Swim the rapids,
Take a chance
By closing your eyes
And following that eye,
Which lurks,
Deep within your mind.

# INSPIRATION

Where lifetime's hopes and dreams like tinder lie,
Our thoughts constrained between two narrow lines,
Ambition pressed beneath a weighted sky,
We find our fragile confidence declines,

Yet find that moment where daylight breaks,
That single spark with which to conjure light,
Where darkness flees and weary self awakes,
Our spirits lift, and mind and soul unite,

For inspiration has at its heart a fact,
That where our truthful words and deeds connect
Where we, renewed, do promise and then act,
We free ourselves to live without regret:

So come, stir your embers, ignite our fire,
And with a single honest spark, inspire

# TRUST

Trust is like an echo
It returns to whence it came
And if you dare not speak it
You will never hear its name

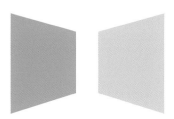

# BEAUTIFUL
# MISTAKES

We made a mistake
A beautiful mistake
A simple inadvertence
Which confirmed
Our humanity
Yet what a liberation
To revel in our imperfection
Let us shout it out aloud
"We tried and failed"
But together we learned
And with such confidence
We renew our vows
To change our world
With smiles upon our faces
And our hearts
Upon our sleeves

## FRIENDLY FIRE

When setting out
To praise,
To celebrate,
Or glorify,
Take heed, that
From the moment
Words depart your lips,
That they will detonate
On friendly ground,
Unseen, and
Unintentioned,
Leaving casualties
In their wake.

## SHE ONLY SAW
## THE LIGHT

She lived in a contented world
Always seeing the best,
Drawing people to her smile,
To her innocence,
But time took its toll,
The crocodile's ticking clock
Eventually catches us all,
Yet laughter, love and happiness
Drowned out the ticks,
For a woman,
Who only ever,
Saw the light.

# YOUR WORD

Not many swear an oath and keep their word
Yet you held it through a lifetime
And stretched it to a way of life.

# MILESTONES

Your joy is difficult to comprehend
For those of us who measure ambition
Through university degrees,
Employment, marriage, homes,
The trappings of a future life,
Everything facing forwards,
A uniform certainty of hope.
Yet in your orbit
That same future presents
A darkened horizon,
Better avoided,
And so you take pleasure
From his presence,
From his very being,
Freed from the milestones
That mark others' journeys.
You accept the moment,
Accept your difference,
But we carry on
With our obsession,
Locked into the future,
Ticking off the boxes,
The place names
On our children's route march,
Too busy to notice
That you can simply enjoy
The person as they are,
Their perfect imperfection,
Living in the here and now,
Enhancing life by living,
By being simply who they are,
Not what they will become.

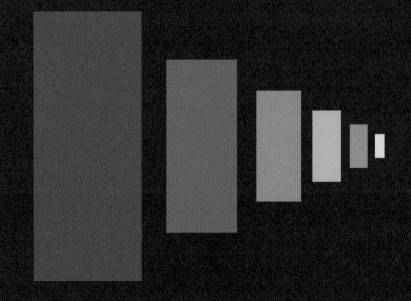

# A MAP IS NOT THE TERRITORY

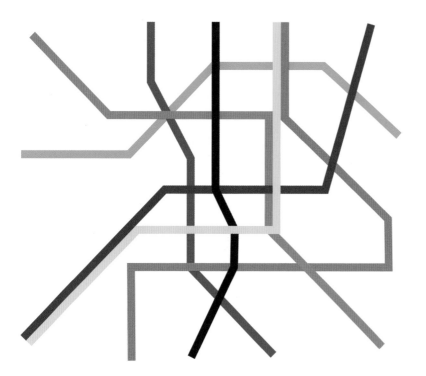

I have a map
Tucked into the back of my mind
Which tells me where I am,
Placing me securely
In my own land,
Triangulating
My position,
But my map
Is not your map,
For our abstractions
Of reality are
Aligned to different poles,
Our choice of scale
Changing everything,
Our intersecting routes
Meeting and departing,
Leaving each behind,
But walk with others ,
Side-by-side
And come to understand,
That we are fellow travellers,
With no monopoly
On place,
So remember this,
There are more maps,
Of our territory,
Than the one we carry
Tucked into the back
Of our minds.

# WHATEVER
# NORMAL IS?

Forget convention and routine,
Escape from commonplace,
For none of us are standard
And average leaves no trace,
We each are an exception,
We are different and unique,
There is no blueprint to us,
We each have our mystique,
So fight back against temptation
To regress towards the crowd,
Stand up for who we are,
And shout it out aloud,
And if we fear rejection,
We must remember this,
That none of us are normal,
Whatever normal is?

# SEEING FOR OURSELVES

We ought never forget
The feelings of the many, who
Only judge by the chill
Upon their collars, nor should we
Stand too close to the edge, when warm
Hands are placed behind our backs, or
Forget to listen to those who never speak, but
Who shake their heads, when
Others leave the room, alternatively,
Forget them all, and
Have faith in our inner child, who
Sees things as they really are.

# WHO DID YOU PLAN TO BE?

Who did you plan to be?
Did you fall far from your tree
Of hope and expectation?
Were you carried off
Swept out to sea, or
Blown far by a cruel wind?
Were you cast adrift
Struggling against the tides?
Or did you take advantage
Of the updraughts?
Did you catch a fair wind,
Fill your sails,
And plane across the surface,
The spray on your cheeks,
And sun on your back?
Yet unexpected destinations
Await us all.
For some,
These rot us from within,
Until our very presence
Becomes unwelcomed,
Whilst others smile
Happy to be on the journey,
Making the most,
Of tides and prevailing winds,
Turning life to advantage,
And turning it,
To gold.

# SCALES OF IMAGINATION

Brass they were,
Elegantly precise,
Engineered from another age
With a pendulum balanced
On a knife edge of reason
And there,
Without catching my eye,
She placed a single fact
In a flat-bottomed dish
And a single dream in the other,
And after a moment's,
Hesitation,
The balance tipped
To the dream.

# REMEMBERING
# THE FUTURE

Think forwards,
Remember that time
When your dreams
Come true, and eternal
Hopes have sprung,
Recall the very moment
When tomorrow
Becomes today,
As you travel
Through time,
Backwards and forwards,
Forwards and backwards,
In transitory thoughts
Of who you were,
And what you might yet
Become,
For now is always
Destined to be the
Past,
And, with that in mind,
Throw off
The shackles of the
Present,
And fulfil your
Obligation,
For tomorrow,
Today

# I AM A FORTRESS

I have a secret that sits in my dreams, squeezing out of my sleep, tempting my screams. For I have a secret that clings to my back, weighing me down like stones in a sack. Yet I am a fortress. My walls never breached. My heart is an island. My soul never reached. I stay in the present, not a glance to the past. I keep on the move and like travelling fast, avoiding reflections, or looking too deep, preferring instead to always compete. For I know I am better, than all you combined. My will is undaunted. I will leave you behind. Propelling me forwards to where I don't know. But my journey has started and to them I will show, that I have succeeded, for that is a fact. Yet the boy deep within me feels muffled and trapped. So deep in the night, when my walls they depart, and I'm no longer able to shelter my heart. My doubts and my feelings they rush to the fore, and I know that I cannot pretend anymore. So let me admit, to all who can hear. That I am no fortress, of that let's be clear. Please help me remove my walls and my fences, and let me take down my remaining defences, and let me live life as the boy from my youth, for the journey I'm on has strayed far from the truth.

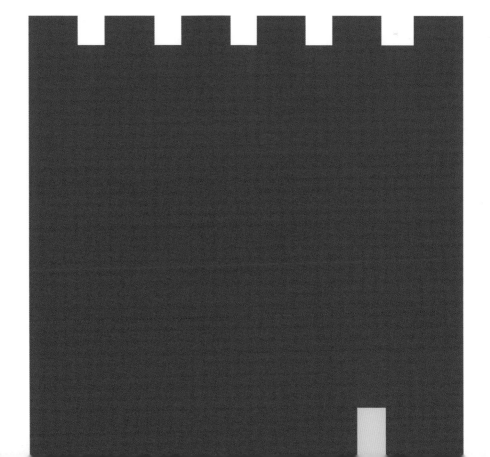

# A FORCE OF NATURE

She, as if possessed by nature's gods
Can turn our very darkness into light;
And lift sagging spirits against the odds,
Where by fervent charge she leads the fight.

True to herself, her soul, like starlight shines,
To guide our lifetime's course between the rocks;
A shining light which integrity defines,
Stretching our minds beyond their narrow box.

But she would not wish our uninvited praise,
Nor expect our acclamation or reward;
Nor seek to waste remaining autumn days,
By polishing memories which others hoard.

Instead, she lives by everlasting truth,
This enchanting woman,
Of perpetual youth.

## ARE YOU THE BEST FRIEND
## THAT YOU COULD HAVE?

Are you the best friend
You would want to have?
To be the one who's with you,
In good times and bad?
Would you forgive,
Would you approve?
Would you stand by you
When others would move?
Are you the person
To cover your back?
Protect you from harm
When under attack?
Would you be there
To listen to your cries?
Would you be honest
And tell you no lies?
Could you share your success
And smile when you win?
Would you forgive
If you'd fallen to sin?
Or are you the kind
Of fair-weather friend
Who cannot be trusted
To be there at the end?
Preferring instead
To come and to go,
Too locked up in yourself
To be able to show?
So, would you be with you,
Through good times and bad,
And could you be the best friend,
That you'd ever have?

# FEAR OF
# MY LIGHT
# GOING OUT

I have a fear,
A deep sustaining fear,
That my light goes out
That my sense of joy and wonder
Which shines upon
The darkest corners
Of my world
Goes out,
Extinguished,
Like a guttering candle
By the whistling draughts,
To leave the
Desolate darkness
Free to cast
Its blackening gloom
Upon my soul

# TO SEE OURSELVES

We only see our gaps
Our defects and deformities
Our slightest flaws
Amplified by the dark
Morning hours
Which break like waves
Across our dreams
Pulling us back
Towards the depths.
But step back
Look out instead from
Watching eyes who
See our wonder
The magic in our hands
That special touch
Which others notice
But escapes our eye
Too busy digging
Our defences
To see ourselves,
As others see us.

# THE CHIEF EXECUTIVE

Do not confuse the man with his position
Nor his possessions for the man
For behind the eyes the boy remains,
Carrying his past with pride,
No shameful burden here,
But a rock from which to launch himself
Upon an unsuspecting world,
Powering him through waters
Where others sadly fail,
A ship indeed,
Welcoming on board
His fellow travellers
To join a lifetime's journey
And never cast ashore,
His quiet gift, unseen at first,
Sees others as his equal,
Regardless of their rank or role,
But wary here,
Do not treat lightly,
Or take him for a fool,
For forgiveness is unlikely
If that bond of trust might fail,
Yet watch him to the rescue
When others lose their feet,
To catch them on the stumble
Without needing to be seen,
But feel the steel, the core, the heart,
The courage, and the edge,
The knack to make decisions
Where others fear to tread,
His joy of life, his bond, his word,
His willingness to give,
Are all but simply facets
Of a many-sided man,
But at his heart, his soul,
The very driver of his being,
The boy behind the eyes remains
With family at his core.

# TUGGING AT A
# LOOSENED THREAD

Feel the tug,
At the loosened thread,
Pulling you back,
To that place,
That place you
Fought so long to escape,
That feeling of entrapment,
Security and safety,
It's very smallness
Of mind and space,
Its traditions,
Its knowingness,
The very things,
Which clawed at your neck,
Closing their fingers,
Taking your breath,
Pushing you away,
Now call out your name,
Tugging at the loosened
Thread, and you come,
Unable to explain,
And all the while,
The thread,
Tightens,
Holding you,
Man and boy,
Forever.

## BETTER TO BE ROUGHLY RIGHT

It took an economist of all people
To point out the folly of precision
Our desire to pin things down
To a singularity
A statement of truth
A distilled certainty
From our confusions
So we spend our time
Constantly flicking
To the back of the book
Searching out the answer
For that imprecise precision
Choosing to ignore
That it is
Better to be
Roughly right
Than precisely
Wrong

# BELONGING

Befriended by his thoughts,
His self certainty
Freed him from a coupling world,
Disconnecting him,
With no desire to belong,
To needlessly attach himself
To flotsam floating on the seas,
Which left untouched
Would disappear from sight,
Carried by the tide
To other castaways;
For bonds were binds
That tied him down,
Limiting his choice,
Narrowing his view,
Constraining him
From his task,
So unencumbered,
He climbed the rungs,
In single-sided mutuality;
And so he came to lead,
As he had lived,
Seeing others as the parts,
And 'drove' his machine,
Forcing it, compelling it,
Watching its momentum,
But missing the people,
Who, gradually,
Separated themselves,
By looking at their feet
Detaching, drifting,
Protecting themselves,
Then looking inwards,
Letting go,
Until he stumbled,
And screamed for their support,
Where none would come,
Leaving him to fall to earth,
Wide-eyed, and
Alone

42

# THE ANALYST

The dark lumpen mass,
Lay anchored to the ground
Defined by brutish bulk,
Men threw themselves at it,
Attempting to lift it whole,
Showing off their strength,
But it beat them all,
Defying all-comers,
Until the waif-like figure
Struggled to the front,
Pausing before the scene,
Respecting the scale,
She barely touched it,
Loosening its grip,
Teasing one small part at a time,
And gradually it gave itself to her,
Revealing its incoherent parts,
And she reduced them,
One by one,
Dissecting and eliminating,
Partitioning and reasoning,
Visualising another form,
Creating in her mind,
Rebuilding the connections,
Moving gradually,
From knowing nothing,
To knowing what,
To knowing how,
Until the final insight,
Knowing,
Why.

# THE DIFFERENCE BETWEEN
# KNOWING AND UNDERSTANDING

Listening to those
Who quote at length
Drop names and dates
To prove their point,
Underlining their
Credentials,
By marking the territory,
Leaving their scent,
Diminishing not enhancing
With each and every text,
Wielding their booklist
As a Weapon
Of  Mass Instruction;
Forcing those of us
To blankly nod in wonder,
At faceless names
Lined up behind them
As Reinforcements
Claiming the ground,
Until the day I met
A man, a wise and quiet man
Who once was told,
"Nicholas, you know nothing,
Yet you understand
Everything"
Let me stand beside
That man in homage
To those who simply seek
The truth from learning
And when they find it
Share it quietly,
No bludgeoning
Force required.

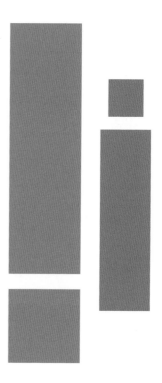

# THE LEADER'S SACRIFICE

Bare your back,
Accept the blows
Which come your way,
Receive them gratefully
On behalf of those
You serve,
Sheltering behind
Your shield,
Absorbing their pain,
But beware,
The blackness
Of the dark hours
Extract their toll,
One dream,
After another,
After another,
Unless, renewed,
By future's hope,
The breaking of a dawn,
Carrying you forwards
Towards a time
Inhabited by light,
Where doubts expire,
And people see it
For themselves,
And step beyond,
Your guard,
To freedom's
Choice.

# THE TIME
# BORROWER

He used to borrow time,
Picking it from the pockets
Of his future self;
Burdening the other him
With those tasks that
He preferred to avoid;
Pushing everything
Into tomorrow's
Hidden crevices;
Spending his inheritance,
Piling up the debt,
Until that moment
When he became
That future self,
And even then,
Despite the evidence,
The need to accept
His delegated burden;
He pushed it on again,
Ignoring the consequences.
Living beyond his means;
The deadline, racing now,
Towards him, eating time
From the other side;
Leaving nothing left to borrow,
And the future self,
Broken and ignored,
Confronts himself
Hurtling forward
From the profligate past,
The time borrower
Coming to pay his
Final debt.

# UNCERTAINTY

I have a doubt,
A doubt that releases,
Me from certainty,
A doubt that I hold
To be self-evident,
Yet hidden from view,
A doubt that
Comes as joyous daybreak,
From the bonds
Of infallibility,
So say it first, softly,
Quietly,
With pride,
"I know not what to do"
Allow your words
To break upon the shore,
Free at last,
Free at last.

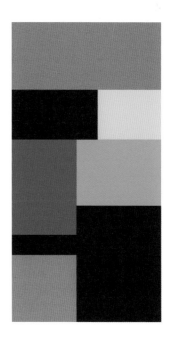

# VULNERABLE INVULNERABILITY

Meet those people impervious to pain
Confidence piled upon confidence
Looking beyond your shoulder
For the next more interesting
Person to enter the room
But watch, when no one watches
See them seeking confirmation
Seeking out the affirmation
That their climb has been worthwhile
But do not fall prey to easy pity
They cannot see it for themselves
And only in that time somewhere in the future
Will regret sweep all away before it
Revealing their folly of living in the present
And the fleeting riches of the fool.

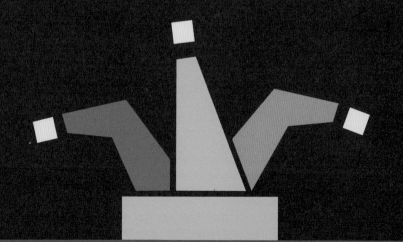

# ADAPTABILITY

The chameleon
Shifts it skin
Through the rainbow,
Travelling unnoticed
Through life,
Merging against
Time's background,
Safe from sight,
Yet even it,
Protected from plain view,
Requires to stand
Its ground
At times,
Declaring
"This is me"
Not hiding
But shouting
"I choose"
"To be"
"Myself"

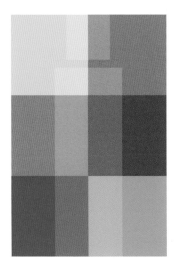

# WAVES AGAINST THE WIND

We are waves against the wind
And have two ways to reach the shore
By keeping low we hide behind
The crashing waves that lead the blind
But those who dare to rise and fight
And lead the charge in selfless flight
Can bear their chests against the storm
Their silver manes give god-like form
They shout and roar their battle cry
Whilst lifting up their pennants high
Of danger they need take no heed
And live their lives at reckless speed
On reaching shallows stand their height
Before they drop their heads mid-flight
And crash and die and live no more
Amidst those of us who slide ashore.

# AN
# INCONVENIENT
# TRUTH

Turn away,
Turn inside,
Stay within your world,
Ignoring,
Removing from your presence
The inconvenient truth,
Which magnifies your lie,
Intruding upon your comfort,
Waking you,
In the middle
Of the black, black night,
Breaching your walls.
So you sleep
And lie,
Waking and sleeping,
Simultaneously,
Choosing to trust
In a more
Convenient 'truth',
And blaming those,
Who dare to share
The dark reality,
Upon which you wish
To draw a shroud.

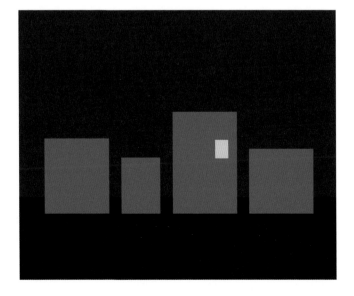

# LEADERSHIP:
# POETRY OR PLUMBING

"Are you a poet
Or a plumber?"
The old woman asked,
And for a moment
I was lost,
By her simplicity,
Trapping me,
Forcing me towards
One side or the other,
And then she smiled,
Opening a door
On the reality,
That we must
Embody
Both.

**CEANNAS**™
■■■■■ MEANS LEADERSHIP

**Ceannas** has a vision to become a 100-year-old company focused on helping leaders to make a long-term, sustainable impact on the organisations they lead and the world in which we live.

**Ceannas is the Scottish Gaelic word for leadership.**

**The Ceannas Curve**© depicts our approach where we enable leaders to identify and

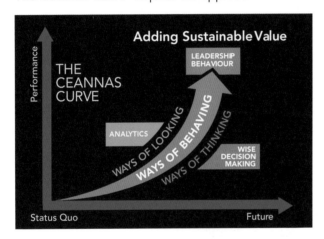

make small, yet exponential, changes to their leadership behaviour, by adopting new 'ways of looking' at themselves as leaders, and new 'ways of thinking' about leadership as a 'wise leader'.

The title of this book, "The only true wisdom is knowing that you know nothing" is ascribed to Socrates. The 'Socratic Paradox' lies at the heart of what it is to be a wise leader.

It is our sincere hope that some of the poems in this book will have a personal resonance for the reader and in so doing encourage them to think about how they might make a productive shift in their own behaviour.

If you'd like to find out more about our work, please visit our website at www.ceannas.com

## Don Ledingham

Don Ledingham is Chief Executive of Ceannas. All the poems that appear in this book have been written by Don over the last eight years and have emerged from his work with individual leaders and organisations around the world.

**DESTI>**
**NATION**
CREATE

**Destination Create** is a brand communication company. They help organisations discover and define what makes them unique and special, creating propositions, messaging and imagery designed to promote their distinctive brands.

Its principals, Gary Haston and Derek Ritchie, have worked with Ceannas since its inception, creating and designing differentiating communication and training material that champion the unique Ceannas approach to leadership training and development.

The Ceannas process of enabling leaders make a series of small changes, leading to an exponential improvement in performance, formed the basis of the original "Ceannas: Leadership by Design" identity. The Fibonacci Spiral perfectly reflects this process. Using the spiral as their inspiration, the designers then added colour and shape to render their own dynamic, geometric version of the form.

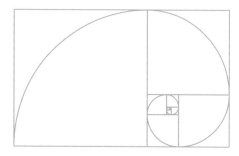 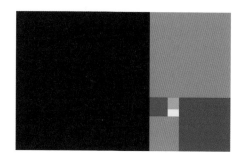

The seven colours and shapes used in this identity now run throughout the majority of Ceannas brand and communication material. Supporting this fascinating body of poetry are illustrations created by Gary Haston following that same visual route.

Sometimes mesmerising, sometimes intriguing, always thought-provoking.